SOUTH AFRICA

UNPACKED

Published in 2015 by Wayland
Copyright © Wayland 2015

Wayland
338 Euston Road
London NW1 3BH

Wayland Australia
Level 17/207 Kent Street
Sydney, NSW 2000

Editors: Annabel Stones and Elizabeth Brent
Designer: Peter Clayman
Cover design by Matthew Kelly

Dewey number: 968'.068–dc23

First published in 2014 by Wayland

ISBN 978 0 7502 8844 6

Printed in China

10 9 8 7 6 5 4 3 2 1

Picture acknowledgements: All images, including cover images and graphic
elements, courtesy of Shutterstock except: p5 © Charles O'Rear/Corbis (l);
© Kim Sayer/Arcaid/Corbis (r); p7 © iStock/Stuart Fox (t); p9 © Onne van
der Wal/Corbis (b); p10 © iStock/duncan1890; p11 © AFP/Getty Images (t); ©
iStock/EdStock2 (b); p12 © Getty Images; p14 © MiKE HUTCHiNGS/Reuters/
Corbis; p18 © David Murray and Jules Selmes; p21 © Getty Images (t); © Forest
Woodward (b); p24 © Michael S. Lewis/CORBIS; p26 © Ian Trower/JAI/Corbis;
p29 © James Sparshatt/Corbis (t); © iStock/THEGIFT777 (b)

The website addresses (URLs) included in this book were valid at the time of
going to press. However, it is possible that contents or addresses may
change following the publication of this book. No responsibility for any such
changes can be accepted by either the author or the Publisher.

Wayland is a division of Hachette Children's Books, an Hachette UK company.
www.hachette.co.uk

Contents

South Africa: Unpacked

Welcome to the Republic of South Africa - the country at the southernmost tip of the continent of Africa. Brimming with astonishing scenery, history and wildlife, South Africa is one of the richest and most powerful nations on the continent. So, if you want to learn about the world's deepest gold mines, grab the key facts about South Africa's sporting glories or find out about the country's extraordinary cuisine, you've come to the right place!

Fact File

Flag:

Area: 1,219,090km²
Population: 48,601,000 (July 2013 est.)
Capital cities: Pretoria, Cape Town and Bloemfontein
Land Borders: 4,862km with six nations
Currency: The Rand

South Africa

Useful Phrases

Howzit - A common greeting, a mix of 'Hi' and 'How are you?'

Boet - Brother, used as a term of affection

Kif - Cool or great

Now-now - Something that will happen soon

Fundi - An expert or knowledgeable person

Robot - Traffic lights

Hamba kahle - Goodbye in the Zulu language

Totsiens - Goodbye in Afrikaans language

CITY PASS

CITY PASS

King Proteas (national flower)

Springbok (national animal)

Kimberley was the first town in the southern hemisphere to install electric street lights in 1882.

The Goat Tower is literally that — a tall tower with steps for a group of Swiss mountain goats, owned by South African farmer Charles Back, to give them mountain-style exercise!

Three Capitals

South Africa is an unusual country in a number of ways, one of which is that it has not one, not two, but three capital cities, each for a different branch of government: Cape Town (law makers), Bloemfontein (the courts) and Pretoria (for the executive and president). Amazingly, none of these are its biggest city. That title goes to Johannesburg, with over 4.4 million people living in its metropolitan area.

Spectacular Cape Town

Lying between the 1,084.6m high Table Mountain and the coast of the Atlantic Ocean, Cape Town's spectacular location makes it a popular tourist destination. More than 20 million people have taken a cable car ride from the city up to the top of Table Mountain. Others visit the world-famous Kirstenbosch Botanical Gardens at the base of the mountain – home to a staggering 22,000 species of home-grown plants. Cape Town is a major seaport and centre of industry. With over 3.7 million people living in its metropolitan area, it's the country's second largest city.

A cable car takes up to 65 passengers on a 704m climb to the top of Table Mountain.

Quiet and peaceful Bloemfontein, the city where J.R.R. Tolkien, author of *The Hobbit* and *Lord of the Rings*, was born.

Pretty Pretoria

Founded in 1855 by Marthinus Pretorius, the city is the centre of South Africa's government including the President, whose home is in the giant Union Buildings. These were built in 1913 and feature a clock tower with the same chimes as Big Ben in London. Located 50km north of Johannesburg, Pretoria is known as the Jacaranda City for the thousands of colourful purple jacaranda trees which are in bloom in October.

Blooming Bloemfontein

Bloemfontein is located on the edge of high dry grassland. True to its name, which means 'fountain of flowers' in Dutch, its streets are lined with thousands of rose bushes. Bloemfontein is home to the country's Supreme Court and a large business district. It's also the closest major city to Lesotho, an independent nation completely surrounded by South Africa that is ruled by King Letsie III.

 The mighty Union Buildings took 3 years to construct out of granite, concrete and 14 million bricks!

NO WAY!

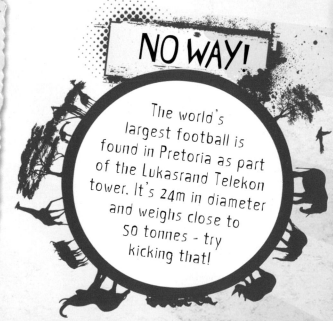

The world's largest football is found in Pretoria as part of the Lukasrand Telekon tower. It's 24m in diameter and weighs close to 50 tonnes - try kicking that!

The Land

South Africa is twice the size of France and five times the size of the UK. A thin strip of low-lying land, mostly between 30 and 240km wide, borders South Africa's long coastline before rising to form a high plateau. This is known as the veld, from the word for 'field' in the Afrikaans language. The veld covers most of South Africa and is divided into different regions based on altitude.

NO WAY!

The Tugela Falls in the Drakensberg mountains feature a massive drop of over 850m - more than six times the height of the London Eye!

 Found in the Drakensberg range, the imposing Sentinel Peak stands 3,166m high.

Highveld and Middleveld

Sitting on ancient rocks, more than 200 million years old, the Highveld contains the mighty Drakensberg mountain range. Here you find most of South Africa's highest peaks, isolated steep-sided hills called kopjes, and rolling grassland. The western part of the plateau is lower than the Highveld and is known as the Middleveld. It is home to many of South Africa's 13 million cattle as well as other livestock raised by ranchers and herders.

 Wildlife flocks to a rare watering hole in South Africa's dry bushveld.

Desert and Bushveld

As you go further west and northwest, the Middleveld's grasslands dry up and all the land becomes desert. Here, the Namib and Kalahari deserts stretch across the border. Temperatures of over 50°C have been recorded in the Kalahari. In the northeast of the country is the Bushveld – an area of lowland wetter and cooler than the Kalahari. Here, trees, bushes and grassy areas support lots of wildlife.

Water Features

Even away from its deserts, South Africa is a largely dry country. Its biggest lake, Lake Chrissie, is 9km long but only 6m deep. The major rivers include the Vaal and the Limpopo, which forms much of the country's boundary with its neighbours Zimbabwe and Botswana. The longest river in South Africa is the Orange, which flows approximately 2,200km westwards from Lesotho to where it forms most of South Africa's border with Namibia.

The Orange River provides water to irrigate the lands of thousands of farmers.

Becoming South Africa

The land that is now called South Africa has been home to African peoples for tens of thousands of years. A number of different African groups, including the Khoekhoen and Nguni people, ancestors of the Zulu and Xhosa, migrated into the region. Dutch farmers, known as Boers, arrived in the 17th and 18th centuries and brought farm workers from Indonesia and India. Further waves of immigrants came from Germany, France and Britain.

Battling for Territory

The 19th century saw many battles and conflicts over land in the region. These were between the European settlers and Africans and between different African groups. Later, the Boers and the British fought two wars (1880-81 and 1899-1902) for control of territories, which the British ultimately won. In 1910, all British territories became the Union of South Africa. Black Africans remained the majority of the population but they now had little land and few rights.

Some of the more than 300,000 British troops involved in the Second Boer War.

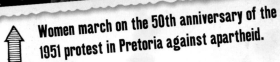
Women march on the 50th anniversary of the 1951 protest in Pretoria against apartheid.

Apartheid

In 1948, the South African government introduced the policy of apartheid. This was racial segregation where black and white people had separate schools, places to eat, parts of trains, even public toilets. The facilities for non-white people were always poorer. Many black people were forced to live in squalid townships outside major cities or in 'homelands' in the countryside, often in areas with few jobs. Protests at this unfairness were sometimes ended violently by armed police.

Nelson Mandela

Nelson Mandela was a black lawyer and campaigner for racial equality who was sentenced to life imprisonment in the early 1960s. For a long time he was held in Robben Island Prison. During his 27 years in jail, he became a worldwide symbol of the struggle against apartheid. Appalled at the violence and injustice shown to black South Africans, many countries refused to either trade with the country or let it take part in major sports and cultural events. In 1989, under a new president, F.W. de Klerk, things changed. Apartheid began to be dismantled, Mandela was released the following year and in 1994, he was elected the first black President of South Africa.

NO WAY!

Nelson Mandela's original cell on Robben Island was barely bigger than him. For much of the time, he was only allowed one visitor a year and the visit lasted just 30 minutes.

Nelson Mandela is considered the 'father of the nation' by most South Africans.

Springbok Sport

During apartheid, sports were segregated, but they are now are something all South Africans can unite and get behind. And how they do! South Africans are sports-mad both as participants and as spectators. They are fiercely proud of the successes of their national sports teams and athletes, and just as proud of hosting many major sporting events including the Rugby, Cricket and Football World Cups.

A Varied Mix

South Africans give almost every sport around a good go, from golf to swimming, cycling, athletics and surfing, and long-distance events from mountain biking to swimming. You'd have seriously sore arms after competing in the 230km long Berg River Canoe Marathon and equally sore legs after taking part in the Comrades Marathon between the cities of Pietermaritzburg and Durban. This 90km-long race attracts around 18,000 runners every year and is longer than two back-to-back marathons!

A cyclist speeds along the 900km of off-road tracks that make up the Old Mutual joBerg2c race.

Cricket and Rugby

South Africa possesses two of the world's leading national teams in cricket and rugby union. The country's national team, known as the Springboks, has won the Rugby World Cup twice (in 1995 and 2007). Its biggest regional sides play against Australian and New Zealand teams in the Super 15s championship every year, which the Bulls, based in Pretoria, have won three times. The South African cricket team, featuring legends such as Jacques Kallis, Graeme Smith and AB de Villiers in 2012, became the first cricket team to be ranked number one in the world in all three forms of cricket: Test cricket, ODIs and Twenty20.

A massive crowd of 94,713 fans watch the 2010 South Africa v New Zealand rugby match at Johannesburg's FNB Stadium.

NO WAY!

In 2005, the South African rugby union team recorded its biggest victory, thrashing Uruguay 134-3!

Footballers compete for the ball in a local match held in Pretoria.

Bafana Bafana

Football was brought to South Africa by British soldiers in the 19th century and is now the country's most popular sport. Millions play it, so you can imagine the joy when the country became the first in Africa to host a FIFA World Cup in 2010. Their national team is nicknamed Bafana Bafana, meaning 'the boys, the boys'. The Premier Division is the top tier of club competition, with teams like the Orlando Pirates and 2013 champions, Kaizer Chiefs, competing.

Farming the Land

South African farms are often either very large or tiny - there's not a lot in between. The largest farms are big businesses rearing vast numbers of livestock (such as sheep, of which the country has 28 million) or producing huge crop yields. At the other end of the scale are single-field farms or small herds of livestock such as goats or cattle. These are tended by the rural poor of South Africa, who scratch out a difficult living.

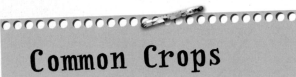

Common Crops

Potatoes are the most common vegetable crop, followed by tomatoes, onions and green mealies (sweetcorn). Sorghum grain is often grown by small farmers whilst rooibos plants are grown to make a hot drink known as bush tea. Near parts of the coast and in the northeast of the country, tropical fruits including pineapples and mangoes are grown, whilst apples and pears are mostly produced in the southwest.

Rooibos tea leaves are only grown in a small area of the country but sold worldwide.

An irrigation system draws up water from a river and then waters farmlands in the Western Cape.

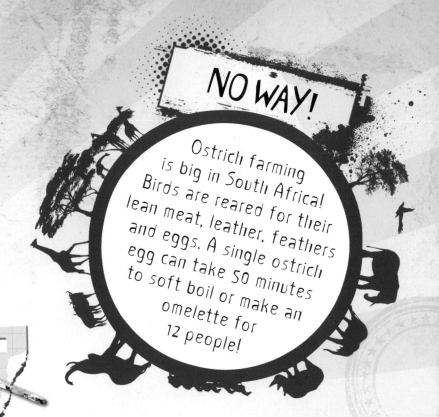

NO WAY!

Ostrich farming is big in South Africa! Birds are reared for their lean meat, leather, feathers and eggs. A single ostrich egg can take 50 minutes to soft boil or make an omelette for 12 people!

Water Shortages

Water remains the South African farming industry's biggest issue. Rivers and large streams are exploited to channel water to fields, a process called irrigation. Around 1.3 million hectares of farmland are supplied with water via irrigation, making up around half of all of South Africa's water consumption. Droughts are a constant fear for owners of farms, big and small. A major drought in 2013 saw many crops fail and some farms abandoned.

Farming Exports

Over half of South Africa's giant crop of oranges and other citrus fruits are sold abroad. The country also has a large, profitable wine industry. In 2013 it processed grapes from over 300 million vines to produce 870.9 million litres of wine. Most of the vineyards are based in the Western Cape region and much of the wine is exported to other parts of the world. Other common exports are sugar cane, peanuts and sunflower seeds.

Vineyards near Cape Town. Around 1.5% of the world's vineyards are in South Africa.

Rainbow Nation

Peoples from many parts of the world have moved to South Africa, settling alongside the different groups of Africans already present. Each has preserved their own cultures, traditions and languages, creating a massive mix that makes South Africa the Rainbow Nation.

Far and Wide

Around 80% of the country's population are black Africans from a wide range of different ethnic groups, including the Zulu, Xhosa, Tswana, Bapedi and Ndebele. The San people live in the Kalahari Desert and are descendants of some of South Africa's earliest inhabitants.

From the East

Around 2.5% of South Africa's population originate from southern Asia. Many of their ancestors were brought over more than 150 years ago to work on plantations or followed later as traders and merchants. Phoenix, a township near Durban, is the largest Indian settlement in South Africa with over 170,000 people.

A Zulu man in traditional dress.

A white South African farmer examines his orange crop in western South Africa.

European Settlers

White South Africans number around 4.5 million. Some are descendants of the Dutch or German colonists who now speak Afrikaans, whilst others hailed from Britain, Portugal, Greece and France and speak their own languages.

Zulu Peoples

Making up around 20% of the population, the Zulu are South Africa's single largest ethnic group. Zulu traditional clothing, sometimes worn on ceremonial occasions, is famous for its beautiful, intricate beadwork.

Mind Your Language

South Africa has a staggering 11 official languages. These are English, Afrikaans, Ndebele, Northern Sotho, Sotho, Swazi, Tswana, Tsonga, Zulu, Venda and Xhosa. The most widely spoken are Zulu, Xhosa and Afrikaans.

Xhosa Common Words
Yebo – Yes
Enkosi – Thank you
Ngiyabonga – I thank you
Kunjani? – How are you?
Kulungile – Good, fine

Zulu Common Words
Ewe – Yes
Cha – No
Ngiyabonga – I thank you
Unjani? – How are you?
Kuhle – Good, fine

A young Tswana girl, one of around 3 million Tswana that live in South Africa.

Fabulous Food

South Africa's many different peoples and cultures have resulted in some fascinating foods as different waves of settlers planted new crops and brought new recipes to the country. Many South Africans eat out at roadside or market stalls or, for those with the money, at fancy city restaurants.

NO WAY!

Mopane worms aren't worms at all. They're giant, ugly caterpillars. Some South Africans squeeze their guts out then dry them or fry them to make a crispy snack!

Mixed Mealtimes

Many dishes mix African ingredients with an Asian influence. This leads to some unusual dishes rarely found elsewhere, such as *kota* or bunny chow (a curry stuffed into a hollowed-out bread loaf), and tandoori crocodile! Spiced fish and rice dishes also came from Asia as does *bobotie*. This looks like a shepherd's pie but the meat is spiced with curry powder, it contains raisins, apples and almonds, and it's topped with egg.

A freshly baked *bobotie*, often eaten with a chilli sauce called Sambal. The first recipe appeared in a Dutch book in 1609.

Eaten for Ages

Some South African dishes are believed to have been eaten long before settlers from Europe arrived and are still part of the diet today. *Mieliepap* is a thick, stiff porridge made from ground maize which is boiled. For many poorer South Africans, this is a staple food, with vegetables or stewed meat sometimes added. You can spice it up with a hot chutney called *chakalaka*, made from carrot, onion, peppers and vinegar. Other traditional dishes are *potjiekos* – large pots of meat and vegetable stews simmered on hot coals or wood fires.

A steaming hot pot of *potjiekos*, left to simmer and rarely stirred.

An outdoor butchers in Soweto prepares fresh meat.

Chewy beef biltong will exercise your jaw muscles.

Meaty Moments

Many South Africans love their meat, from giant beef steaks and lamb chops to wild game such as ostrich, crocodile and antelope. Some meat, particularly beef, is dried and spiced to form a chewy snack called biltong. *Boerewors* are handmade sausages, sometimes spicy, and often rolled into a spiral, whilst *sosaties* are cubes of lamb or mutton marinated in sauce overnight. Many South Africans insist that these meaty treats are best cooked on an outdoor flaming grill similar to a barbecue but called a *braai*.

Rich and Poor

Life varies hugely in South Africa depending on whether you're rich or poor. Over centuries of rule by other countries, much of South Africa's wealth has become concentrated in small numbers of people whilst far greater numbers live in poverty.

Luxury houses perch on a ridge overlooking the sea.

Living in Poverty

Life is incredibly tough for the poorest South Africans in and around the country's cities. Many live in shanty towns, in basic homes without electricity or running water, where crime is common. An estimated 88,000 South Africans make their living as waste pickers, scavenging large rubbish dumps looking for metals and other items they can sell. They face hazards from razor-sharp metals and glass as well as toxic chemicals.

Big Divide

Since the first free elections in 1994, millions more South Africans have access to basic facilities, such as clean water and electricity, but the gap between the richest and poorest people is getting bigger, not smaller. South Africa is home to over 48,000 millionaires and for the wealthy, the country offers amazing opportunities. Yet around a quarter of the country's overall population is unemployed and many millions of people have to live on an income of less than £1 a day.

One-room huts made of corrugated iron sheets in the Soweto township.

Fighting Disease

Many of South Africa's poorest people are at risk from diseases including tuberculosis, Hepatitis A and HIV/AIDS. Approximately 17% of the entire adult population of South Africa is infected with the HIV virus, although over 1.9 million South Africans now receive special drugs to help them live with it.

Patients await treatment at an AiDS clinic in Johannesburg. This small clinic handles around 8,000 patients.

Education

In the past millions of poorer South Africans, who could not afford the fees for private schools, received little education, but the country is now investing greatly in schools. In 2013, 21% of the country's national budget was spent on education, including its higher education colleges and universities such as the University of South Africa. Based in Pretoria and with 350,000 students, it's the largest university on the continent.

Education is compulsory in South Africa between the ages of 7 and 15.

Wild Life

South Africa has an incredible array of creatures including over 240 different mammal species, from aardvarks to zebras. There's also more than 300 types of bird and around 100 different snakes, a quarter of which are poisonous, so watch out! In more recent years, South Africa has taken steps to try to protect some of its more endangered species. For example, there were just 120 elephants in the country in 1920 whereas today there are an estimated 12,000.

At over 19,600km², Kruger National Park is almost as big as Wales.

NO WAY!

You'd expect penguins in Antarctica but not in South Africa! Yet around 40-45,000 African penguins live round the country's coastline.

On Safari

South Africa attracts over 8 million tourists per year. Many of these come to visit the country's national parks to see the wildlife, particularly the 'big five': the lion, the enormous African elephant – which can reach 6 tonnes in weight – the leopard, the rhinoceros and the Cape buffalo.

Tourists in a jeep in a national park take snaps of a large elephant.

National Parks

Habitat loss due to farming, mining and industry plus hunting and pollution had seen some creature numbers plunge alarmingly. Fortunately, attempts have been made to protect many of these creatures and conserve their natural homes. South Africa now has 19 national parks that together cover an area of around 37,000km². In addition to the national parks, South Africa has around 500 smaller protected areas or nature reserves which are also havens for the country's wildlife to thrive in.

Cape Buffalo

Lion

Amazing Animals

The big five are far from the only animal attractions in South Africa. There are loggerhead turtles, the hefty hippopotamus and the world's tallest animal, the giraffe, which can reach 5.5m in height. In addition, there are baboons, vultures, antelope, wildebeest, super-cute bushbabies and the world's fastest land animal, the super-speedy cheetah, which can reach top speeds in the wild of 90km/h.

Rhino

Rhinos and South Africa's big cats are best watched from a distance!

Gold and Diamonds

South Africa's wealth is based on its huge metal and mineral deposits. In the 1880s, the discovery of a rich seam of gold led to the Witwatersrand Gold Rush. Thousands of prospectors flocked to the region, which resulted in the creation of the city of Johannesburg. Since then, gold has been mined in huge quantities along with other metals and coal.

NO WAY!

A third of all the gold in the world today has come from South Africa.

A gold miner drills the rock more than 3km underground at the Savuka gold mine.

Gold Rush

Much of the gold mined today in South Africa comes from deep underground mines. Some mines, such as Mponeng, East Rand and TauTona, are more than 3km deep. Temperatures below ground can reach a sweltering 60°C and the journey back to the surface takes an hour in lifts called cages.

Dazzling Diamonds

In 1867, 15-year-old Erasmus Jacobs found South Africa's first known diamond close to the Orange River. Since then, diamonds have been recovered in enormous quantities. Over 2,700kg of diamonds were mined from the Big Hole mine in Kimberley. At 453m wide and over 210m deep, this is believed to be the biggest hole dug by hand in the world. The world's largest diamond, the Cullinan was discovered in South Africa in 1905. It weighed 3,106.75 carats (1 carat=0.2 grams). To put this in perspective, some 10 carat diamonds sell for over half a million pounds! The Cullinan was shipped to Europe in secret and ended up in the crown jewels of the British Royal Family.

The Big Hole in Kimberley yielded over 14.5 million carats of diamonds.

Mine Time

It's not all gold and diamonds. Iron ore, copper, silver and titanium are also mined, and South Africa is the world's biggest producer of the metals platinum and chromium, both used in industry. Coal is mined in huge quantities and is the main fuel used in South Africa's power stations. And there's enough left over for the country to be one of the world's top five exporters of coal. Gumboot dancing was invented by South African miners. To communicate with each other in deep, dark mines without radios or phones, they stamped their wellies, known as gumboots, in different sequences of signals.

The gigantic Palabora copper mine features a hole that's 2,000m wide.

On the Coast

South Africa has around 2,800km of coastline, with the Indian Ocean on one side and the Atlantic Ocean on the other. The two oceans meet at Cape Agulhas, the southernmost point of both South Africa and the African continent. Whale watching, swimming with dolphins and shark spotting are all popular coastal activities, but the coast also provides important employment for fishermen, port workers and those in the tourist trade.

Surf City

Surfing is a popular pastime along South Africa's coast but nowhere is it more popular than the city of Durban. Nicknamed Surf City, its many surf spots include the Bay of Plenty and Dairy Beach. The city also boasts a stretch of beachfront known as the Golden Mile. Rickshaws were imported from Japan in 1892 and are still used as a form of taxi transport here. Many people who pull the rickshaws dress in traditional Zulu clothing and headdresses to attract business.

One of a handful of Zulu rickshaw drivers in Durban. 100 years earlier, there were over 2,000 of them.

Coastal Industries

Durban is also the country's largest seaport but there are others including Port Elizabeth and Port of Richards Bay. These ports handle vast amounts of trade and shipping – from exports of metals and machinery to China, Japan and the United States (its three biggest trading partners), to imports of food, oil and chemicals. The country's fishing industry catches over 600,000 tonnes a year and is mostly concentrated on its Atlantic coast where large hauls of anchovies, hake and tuna are landed.

Atlantic fishing trawlers' boats dock near Cape Town.

The Sardine Run

Every year between May and August, a mass migration of sardines travels up the east African coast in gigantic shoals. Known as the sardine run, the shoals can be a staggering 7km long and contain millions of fish – which form an appetising all-you-can-eat buffet for seabirds, sharks, dolphins, seals and other marine life. These predators have fast turned the sardine run into a tourist attraction. There's even a telephone hotline you can phone to find out if it's heading your way so you can go and watch.

NO WAY!

Tourists can pay to be lowered in a metal cage into the shark-infested depths of the sea to get up close to the fearsome predator, the Great White Shark.

A Great White shark gets up close and personal with tourists protected by a shark cage.

Holidays and Festivals

If there's one thing that South Africans like, it's a party! Holidays, celebrations and festivals give great opportunities for the population to shout, sing, cheer, dance and take part in annual gatherings.

NO WAY!

At the Whoosh festival in the town of Worcester 70 or so teams all trample grapes in a vat to produce the most juice in a set time.

27th April is Freedom Day and it commemorates the first free democratic elections for all people in South Africa.

21st March is Human Rights Day and recalls the Sharpeville Massacre in 1960 when 69 people were killed and 180 wounded by police fire.

9th August is National Women's Day and remembers the day in 1956 when large numbers of women marched in protest against the apartheid laws.

Time to Eat

Food and drink festivals range from the Soweto Beer Festival to Pretoria's Annual Evergreens Chilli Carnival with the hottest spices around. There's even a festival devoted to dried meat – the Great Biltong Festival in the town of East Somerset.

Tribal Celebrations

Many African groups have their own traditions and festivals, from the annual Xhosa festival at Langa and the Venda people's snake dance around Lake Fundudzi, to the Royal Reed Dance of the Zulus. This sees tens of thousands of Zulus descend on Nogoma, about 350km from Durban, in September. As many as 15,000 young Zulu women, each carrying a reed to symbolise the power of nature, all dance before the Zulu King.

Second New Year

When the original Dutch settlers celebrated New Year's Day, their slaves and servants had to work but were given the next day off. This has developed into a colourful festival in Cape Town which occurs on 2nd January every year and is called Kaapse Klopse or Tweede Nuwe Jaar, meaning 'Second New Year'. It features some 18,000 brightly coloured minstrels with musical instruments or umbrellas parading through parts of the city in front of large crowds.

A collection of colourful minstrels in Cape Town. Awards are given for the best-dressed and best singers.

29

More Information

Websites

http://www.southafrica.net/za/en/landing/visitor-home
The country's official tourism website is packed with information on all of South Africa's major cities and attractions.

http://www.info.gov.za/aboutsa/history.htm
A detailed history of South Africa from the country's official government website.

http://www.krugerpark.co.za/Kruger_National_Park_Wildlife-Travel/Kruger_National_Park_Wildlife.html
A brilliant collection of features about the major wildlife attractions of South Africa.

http://www.iol.co.za/sport
Get all the latest news and details about cricket, football, rugby, athletics and other sports in South Africa.

Apps

The South Africa Travel Guide
A handy travel guide to more than 1,500 places of interest in South Africa, from parks to museums.

Kruger Park Wildlife Book 2.0
View lots of exciting photos of wildlife from South Africa's Kruger Park on your Android enabled device.

Rainbow Languages Language Guide
This app features everyday words and phrases spoken in South Africa's top eight languages including Afrikaans, Xhosa and Zulu.

Movies

Cry Freedom
The Oscar-nominated story of newspaper editor, Donald Woods and his flight from the country.

Invictus
This 2009 feel-good movie starred Matt Damon and Morgan Freeman and is all about Nelson Mandela and the South African rugby union team which won the 1995 Rugby World Cup.

Sarafina!
A powerful musical film about a young girl living in a black township in South Africa during the apartheid regime.

Clips

http://www.youtube.com/watch?v=jgQBoXsxr8w
A 13-minute long documentary provided by the Nelson Mandela Foundation.

http://www.bbc.co.uk/programmes/b00s6bdh
South Africa in Pictures looks at how photographers have captured this varied and exciting nation.

http://www.youtube.com/watch?v=KDfPV8PNROU
Watch many scenes of the landscape and culture in and around Cape Town.

http://www.youtube.com/watch?v=-4xOXzT4MU8
An hour long film about the history of the Zulu Kingdom.

Books

Countries in Our World: South Africa by Alison Brownlie Bojang
(Franklin Watts, 2012)

Discover Countries: South Africa by Chris Ward and Rosie Wilson
(Wayland, 2010)

Graphic Biographies: Nelson Mandela by Bob Shone and Neil Reed
(Franklin Watts, 2009)

Journey to Jo'Burg by Beverley Naidoo
(HarperCollins Children's Books, 2008)

Tree Shaker: The Story of Nelson Mandela by Bill Keller
(Kingfisher Books, 2008)

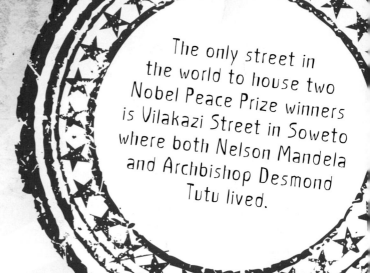

The only street in the world to house two Nobel Peace Prize winners is Vilakazi Street in Soweto where both Nelson Mandela and Archbishop Desmond Tutu lived.

Glossary

Afrikaans A language of South Africa derived originally from Dutch settlers to the region.

altitude The height above sea level, usually measured in metres.

apartheid An old government policy in South Africa of discrimination and separating peoples on the basis of race.

drought A long period with little or no rain, sleet or snow.

exports Goods or raw materials which are sent to another country for sale or trade.

hectare A measure of area equal to 10,000 square metres.

migrated To have moved to a new place.

ODIs Short for One Day Internationals, a type of cricket match played by national teams who each get to bat for 50 overs.

shoal A large group of fish.

staple food A commonly eaten food that forms a major part of people's diet.

township Usually under-developed areas on the edge of cities or towns into which non-white peoples were forced to move under the apartheid system.

unemployed To not have a job and be out of work.

Index